LIQUIDITY

Flowing Forms in Water and Money

by

Stephen Briault and Angus Jenkinson

Tobias Press

What kind of book is this?

~ *Liquidity* is an exploration, in words and pictures, of the dynamics of flow in two contrasting areas of life – water in the natural ecology, and money in the human economy. It draws parallels between these two, which we believe to be more than coincidence or metaphor.

The ideas expressed here describe fundamental gestures or forms which are created out of movement. They are informed by both ancient wisdom and modern philosophy – in particular, the "classical" concept of the four elements – fire, air, water and earth – and the social philosophy of Rudolf Steiner, especially his typology of financial transactions – purchase, loan and gift.

We try to show how the interaction between these fourfold and threefold archetypes manifests itself both in nature and in society.

Building on this, we describe how the current crises, in the capitalist economy on the one hand, and the global environment on the other, show comparable symptoms – debt and drought – and how they both require comparable new thinking to address and potentially heal them.

Levels of manifestation in the natural and social environment

The four classical elements of earth, water, air and fire interact in the natural environment. With water, three relationships immediately appear:

- The flow of water over the earth creates forms in rivers and landscape;
- The action of moving air creates waves on the sea;
- The warmth of the sun produces evaporation and rainfall, fructifying the earth and completing the cycle.

warmth of
the sun

evaporation
& rainfall

air works
on water

air-borne
vapour

wind-blown
moving waves

flow: standing waves

Earth's
landscape
shaped by
water

$ In the case of money:

- Earthly substance is transformed into products which flow from producers to consumers, mediated by money which flows in the opposite direction;

- Relationships between people (although often obscured by institutions and "capital markets") arise through purchase, lending, borrowing and repayment;

- Learning and development is enabled by freeing resources from the economic cycle, to enable the gift of education and culture.

enlivening culture

gift transfers

loans & repayments

economic relationships

money

purchases

nature transformed

Water flows throughout the biosphere, making life possible.

It surrounds and permeates every species and organism.

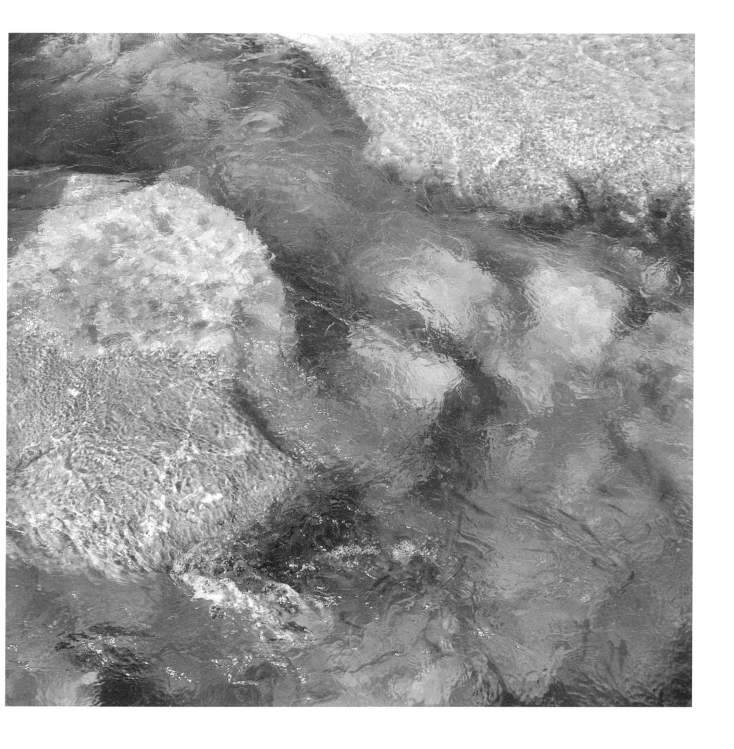

$ Money flows throughout human civilisation, making the global economy possible. It surrounds and permeates every organisation and affects every individual.

Water can penetrate and sustain all forms of life because of its limitless adaptability. It is the only chemical that occurs naturally in all three physical states – solid, liquid and gaseous. It is colourless, odourless, tasteless – sacrificing its own identity for a positive neutrality, to be able to combine with many other compounds and elements.

$ Money can penetrate and support social life because of its adaptability and neutrality. It has no quality of its own, only quantity — but takes on the qualities of a limitless range of transactions, driven by human needs, desires and decisions. Money's neutrality allows it to be used for the highest and the lowest of purposes, and everything in between.

Water has no life of its own, but is essential to every organism. Its movement transfers life-potential between the atmosphere, the subterranean realm and the Earth's surface.

$ Money has no value in itself, but enables the creation, transfer and consumption of economic value. Its movement circulates value from the past, in the present and for the future.

As it moves, water interacts with each of the other elements – earth, air and warmth. These work with it to produce distinct forms and patterns, visible as shapes, waves and clouds.

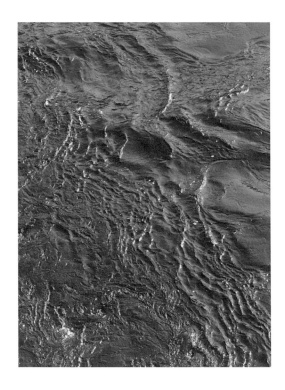

$ As it moves, money interacts with social structures and forms of accounting – profit and loss, balance sheets, and final entries. These make its movements and pauses visible and manageable.

Consolidated Balance Sheet, IFRS

EURm	Note	Dec 20xx	Dec 20xx
Assets			
Property, plant and equipment		6,053	
Investment property		6,765	3,487
Intangible assets		7,012	68
Investments in associates		64	34
Financial assets			
Investments related to unit-linked insurance contracts		531	
Tax assets		5,653	
Reinsurers' share of insurance liabilities		512	527
Other assets			
Cash and cash equivalents		30,222	29,859
Total assets			
Liabilities			
Liabilities for insurance and investment contracts		19,796	13,945
Liabilities for unit-linked insurance and investment contracts		1,034	2,387
Financial liabilities		2,755	
Tax liabilities		432	640
Provisions		37	34
Employee benefits		98	405
Other liabilities		960	1,704
Total liabilities		21,187	20,365
Equity			
Share capital		98	98
Reserves		99	1,530
Retained earnings		1,531	6,459
Other components of equity		6,844	
Equity attributable to owners of the parent		447	8,886
Non-controlling interests		8,920	0
Total equity		0	8,886
Total equity and liabilities		8,920	29,851
		30,107	

Water moves in cycles through the environment – on the land, in the seas and lakes, and through the sky. The cycle of flow, evaporation and precipitation brings about a process of continual purification and renewal, making the same molecules available repeatedly to all life-forms.

$ Money moves in cycles through the economy – in cash, credit and repayment. The cycle of purchase, loan and gift could bring about a process of continual adjustment and renewal, making the same money available repeatedly to all social forms.

··

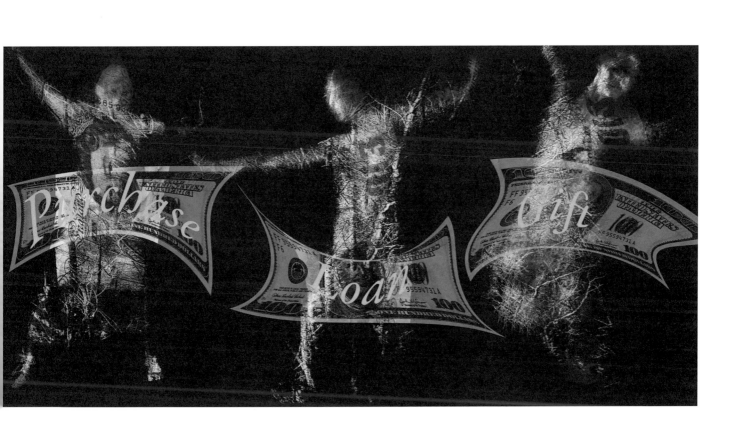

Water has a tendency to form globular shapes, for example in raindrops or hailstones.

$ Money has a tendency to be self-referential,

for example in the "promise" expressed on a UK bank note.

....

When water meets solid land, its movements are pulled by gravity, producing valleys, rivers, and shapes that remain relatively constant, whilst continuously new liquid moves through them. The dynamic relationship of earth and water creates "standing waves" whose forms gradually change with variations in the flow.

$ When money is used to enable the sale and purchase of products and services, an imprint of these transactions appears in bank statements and in income and expenditure accounts. Over time, relatively stable patterns emerge which are summarised in monthly, quarterly or annual accounts. These patterns change gradually from one period to another with variations in prosperity and behaviour.

In large bodies of water, the pull of the moon creates tides, and the movement of the air creates waves. In both cases, the water moves in a cycle and then returns close to its original position. Waves on the open sea, driven by the wind, appear to move across the surface, but what actually happens is that the water molecules themselves move in an up-and-down or circular motion as the wave passes through them. The form moves, but the substance only oscillates.

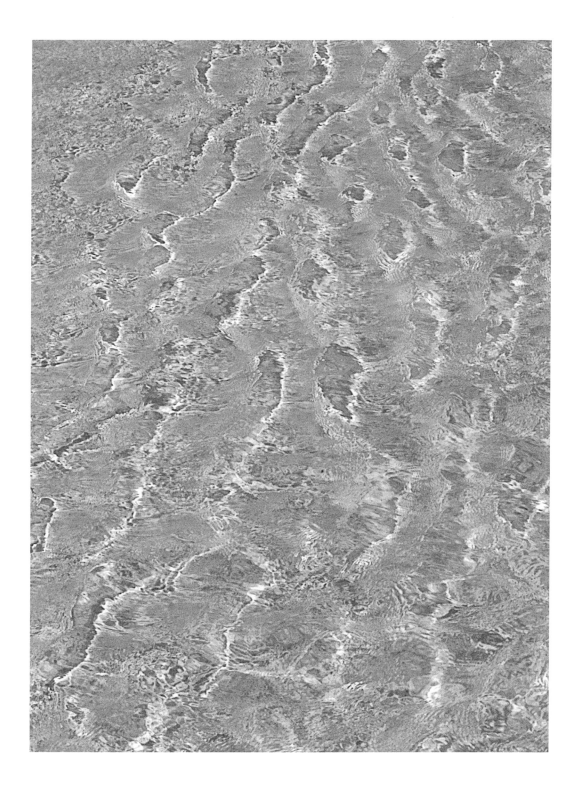

$ Accumulations of money, not currently needed for purchase transactions, form pools of assets that are available for lending. This money enables movement of goods and services, but must always ultimately return to its source, so that the loan fund preserves its value. Lending is driven by the airy, intangible assessment of risk and reward. The economy stagnates when confidence abates: storms arise when the gales of speculation rage too freely.

Life on land is made possible by rain. Through evaporation, water vapour is released from the seas, purified of the compounds it has dissolved, and carried over the land as cloud. Rain is the gift of the sea to the land, supporting plants, animals and humans before returning to the oceans to start the cycle once more.

$ The gift economy supports the fulfilment of human and social potential and renewal. Education, healing, science and arts consume economic resources without offering any immediate return. Yet each reciprocates disproportionately through the benefits of creativity, innovation, discovery and meaning to the ecology of society.

The gift of rainfall has been abused. Rivers and aquifers in many parts of the world have been polluted. Drought and desertification are spreading. Ecosystems, especially wetlands, have been and are being destroyed. One-eighth of the world's population lacks access to clean water supplies.

$ Money flows are abundant in some parts of global society, scarce in others. About one-sixth of humanity lives on less than $1 per day, and every year about 18 million people (50,000 per day) die from poverty-related reasons, mostly women and children. The U.N. has estimated the cost of ending world hunger at about $195 billion a year. In comparison, worldwide military expenditure reached $1,531bn in 2011, up 50% from 2000. Money is used to buy both goods and evils.

What has happened to the rain? 10,000 years ago, the Sahara was a jungle, until it was cleared by humans. Trees both attract and recycle rainfall: when they are cut down, the land dries out. The rain falls back into the oceans instead of enlivening the land.

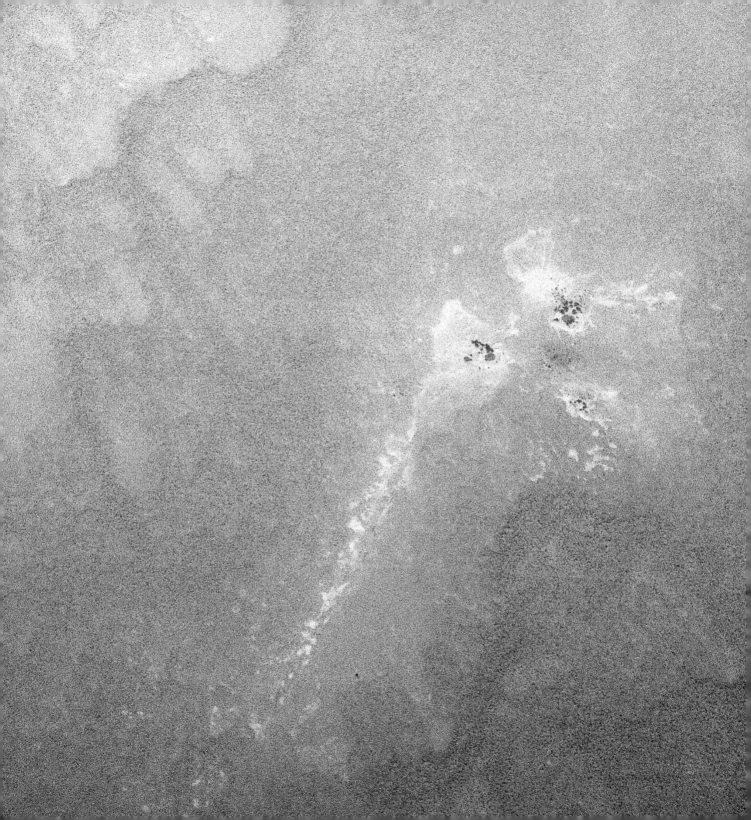

$ Investments are continually recycled: compound interest produces exponential growth of assets – loans that are never allowed to become gifts. Trading in financial "products" now vastly exceeds the real economy. Money makes money out of money, creating profit without creating value, enriching speculators whilst further impoverishing those without investable assets.

Global Transaction Volumes, 2010

Currency exchange & speculation $955 trillion

Financial derivatives $601 trillion

Stocks & shares $87 trillion

Real economy $63 trillion

Source: Hawranek, Dieter et al., Out of Control: The destructive power of financial markets, Der Spiegel-on-line, 22 August 2011.

The accelerating water crisis in our physical environment mirrors the financial crisis in our world economy. Radical, transformational steps need to be taken in both realms – conservation, reforestation, detoxification, healing, rethinking, redesigning the systems, which we create and inhabit, respecting the water of life and the spirit of creativity and compassion.

How do you respond?

Visit the website at www.angusjenkinson.com/liquidity. Hashtag #liquidityforms

liquidity2015@gmail.com

Liquidity: Flowing Forms in Water and Money.

Copyright images and design © Angus Jenkinson, 2015

Copyright text © Stephen Briault, 2014.

First Edition, 2016.

Text is set in Arno Pro.

Cover image and design by Angus Jenkinson.

Published by Tobias Press, Pear Tree House, Priory Road, Forest Row, RH18 5HP, England.

Print format ISBN 978-0-9555362-3-6

eBook format ISBN 978-0-9555362-4-3

Printed by Lightning Source.

© 2014, 2016

Lightning Source UK Ltd.
Milton Keynes UK
UKRC01n0203030517
300362UK00002B/3